ZOMBIES ON THE LOOSE

Anne Rooney

Copyright © ticktock Entertainment Ltd 2008

First published in Great Britain in 2008 by ticktock Media Ltd,
2 Orchard Business Centre, North Farm Road, Tunbridge Wells, Kent, TN2 3XF

ticktock project editor: Ruth Owen
ticktock project designer: Sara Greasley
ticktock picture researcher: Lizzie Knowles

With thanks to series editors Honor Head and Jean Coppendale

Thank you to Lorraine Petersen and the members of nasen

ISBN 978 1 84696 706 1 pbk

Printed in China

Picture credits (t=top; b=bottom; c=centre; l=left; r=right):
Dan Callister/ Rex Features: 31r. Nigel Catlin/ FLPA: 27. Corbis: 11 (man). John Daniels/ Alamy: 5r. David Fernandez/
epa/ Corbis: 10. Getty Images: 15. iStock: 21, 22-23, 29, 31c. Mary Evans Picture Library/ Alamy: 19. Darby
Sawchuk/ Alamy: 5l. Shutterstock: OFC, 1, 2, 4, 8, 9, 11 (flames), 12 all, 13t, 13b, 16-17, 22 inset, 31l. SNAP/ Rex
Features: 6. Norbert Wu/ Minden Pictures/ FLPA: 24-25.

Every effort has been made to trace copyright holders, and we apologise in advance for any omissions. We would be
pleased to insert the appropriate acknowledgments in any subsequent edition of this publication.

CONTENTS

ZOMBIES ON THE LOOSE

You watch in horror as half rotted creatures walk towards you.

They moan.

They groan.

These horrifying creatures are **zombies**.

They are coming to eat your flesh...

MOVIES AND LEGENDS

In modern horror movies, rotting zombies climb out of their graves. They hunt and kill people to eat their flesh.

White Zombie

The first zombie movie was made in 1932.
It was called *White Zombie*. In this movie, a factory owner uses zombies as slaves.

**Zombies don't just appear in movies.
There are old legends about zombies, too.**

Hundreds of years ago, people in Europe believed in zombies. These zombies were known as revenants.

People believed revenants climbed out of their graves to seek revenge on their enemies.

Why did people believe in revenants?

Perhaps, because hundreds of years ago, people were sometimes buried alive by accident. If they woke up, it seemed that they had come back from the dead.

A ZOMBIE LEGEND

In the year 1090, two men died in an English village. The men were buried in the village graveyard.

That night, at midnight, the men were seen walking over the hills. They were carrying their coffins on their backs.

The men had become revenants!

Coffin

People in the village started to fall ill and die. The revenants were killing them.

The villagers dug up the dead bodies. They chopped off the revenants' heads and cut out their hearts.

The village was saved!

Heart

This story is an old legend from hundreds of years ago.

But is it possible that zombies exist today?

VOODOO ZOMBIES

Many people in Haiti, in the Caribbean, believe in voodoo.

Voodoo is an old African religion.

Voodoo priestess

In the 1700s, people were taken from Africa to Haiti to work as slaves. The slaves brought their religion with them.

Voodoo sorcerers called bokors create zombies.

Bokors say they use magic to bring zombies back from the dead. The zombies do everything the bokor tells them to do.

A Bokor

MAKING A ZOMBIE

How do bokors turn people into zombies?

1) First, the bokor feeds a living person zombie powder – without the victim knowing.

Zombie powder is made from puffer fish, toads, poisonous tree frogs and dead human bodies.

2) The person dies and is buried.

3) The bokor digs up the body.

4) The bokor says a spell over the dead body. The person comes back to life as a zombie.

5) The bokor feeds the zombie on a special paste made from the plant zombie cucumber.

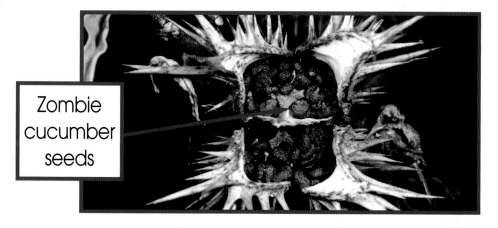

Zombie cucumber seeds

Can a bokor really bring a dead person back to life? Let's look at some real-life zombie stories from Haiti

ZOMBIE SLAVES

Bokors often make zombies to use as slaves. Sometimes they turn an enemy into a zombie as revenge.

In 1918, a bokor named Ti Joseph made a gang of nine zombies.

He made the zombies work in a sugar cane plantation.

Ti Joseph took all the money the zombies earned.

He treated them badly and let them eat only boiled bananas.

15

ESCAPE FROM THE SPELL

Many people believe that zombies must not eat salt or meat. If they do, it makes them realise that they have been turned into a zombie.

Ti Joseph's zombies ate salted nuts.

An explorer called William Seabrook saw this happen. He believed that once the bokor's spell was broken, the zombies realised they were dead. They wanted to go back to their graves. He wrote about what happened:

"The zombies turned toward the graveyard. As their cold hands touched the earth of their own graves, they fell, and lay there, rotting."

FELICIA – THE ZOMBIE

In 1937, something very strange happened in a small village in Haiti.

People saw an old woman walking in the street.
The woman didn't speak.
She didn't seem to know where she was.

One villager thought the woman was a member of their family. They thought the woman was Felicia Felix-Mentor.

Felicia had fallen ill in 1907 when she was 29 years old. She had died and her body was buried.

So how could Felicia be walking through the village 30 years later?

The villagers were frightened.

**There could only be one answer.
Felicia had come back from the dead.
She was a zombie!**

This is a photo of
Felicia Felix-Mentor
in 1937. Was she a
real-life zombie?

"I WAS A ZOMBIE"

A Haitian man named Clairvius Narcisse says he lived as a zombie for two years.

> " I fell ill and died in hospital in 1962.
> I heard my sister crying when I died.
>
> I was buried the next day. I felt the coffin go down into my grave.
>
> Then my body was dug up. A bokor fed me zombie cucumber. He whipped me.
>
> For two years I worked in a sugar cane plantation with other zombies.
>
> In 1964, the bokor died. There was no more zombie cucumber. I got better! "

Clairvius returned to his family in 1982 – 20 years after he died!

21

DON'T BE A ZOMBIE

Some people in Haiti are afraid that they might come back from the dead as a zombie.

To stop this happening, they ask to be buried under heavy stones when they die.

Sometimes the doors of Haitian tombs are locked with a padlock.

Padlock

People believe this will stop a bokor stealing their body to make a zombie.

ARE ZOMBIES REAL?

Can a bokor really make a zombie? Some experts believe that science has the answer.

The Haitian puffer fish contains a deadly poison.
The poison can be made into a powder.

The powder paralyses anyone who takes it.
The person's breathing slows down.
Their heartbeat nearly stops.

The victim seems dead.

But when the poison wears off, they come
back to life.

**Could poison from puffer fish
explain stories of people
coming back from the dead?**

The zombie cucumber is a poisonous plant.

Zombie cucumber can make a person go mad. It can make them forget everything. The person doesn't know what they're doing!

Someone who ate zombie cucumber could be controlled by a bokor.

In Haiti, many people have a strong belief in zombies. When this belief is mixed with strong poisons, it can make a person believe they are a zombie.

A zombie cucumber plant

FELICIA – THE TRUTH

The zombie Felicia Felix-Mentor was examined by a doctor.

The doctor found that the strange woman was not the real Felicia.

He said the zombie-like woman was mentally ill. That was why she didn't speak.

Felicia had been lame before her death. The zombie-like woman couldn't walk very well. Felicia's family thought this was proof it was Felicia. But the woman was just weak from lack of food.

bokor A sorcerer, or magician, who turns people into zombies.

coffin A box that holds a dead body.

grave A hole in the ground where a body is buried.

graveyard A place where many bodies are buried.

lame Unable to walk properly because of an injury to a foot or leg.

legend A story that is passed down through history.

mentally ill A person who has something wrong with their brain.

paralysed Unable to move.

plantation A field or forest where crops are grown.

puffer fish A fish that puffs up its body when it is attacked. Many parts of the puffer fish contain a very strong poison.

revenge To do something bad to someone because they did something bad to you.

slave A person who belongs to another person and has to work for them.

sorcerer Someone who can make magic.

sugar cane A type of grass. Sugar is made from the stems of the grass.

victim A person who is hurt or killed because of an accident or because of something done to them by another person.

voodoo An African religion that involves magic.

Zombie A person who is thought to be dead but is able to walk around.

ZOMBIE SPOTTER'S GUIDE

Revenant
- Lived in Europe hundreds of years ago
- Rotting skin
- Bones sticking out
- Has maggots eating its body
- Carries its coffin wherever it goes

Voodoo zombie
- Lives in Haiti
- Not rotting
- Has normal skin
- Has staring eyes
- It doesn't speak
- Is controlled by a bokor

Movie zombie
- Can live anywhere
- Rotting skin
- Eats human flesh
- Moves slowly but can carry on even if hurt
- Moans and groans

ZOMBIES ONLINE

Websites
http://www.zombiewalk.com/
Find out how to join a zombie walk in your area

http://zombies.tomwalsham.com/costume.html
How to do zombie make-up and costumes

http://zombies.monstrous.com
Information about different types of zombies

INDEX